Great Grills

Wendy Godfrey

SIMON & SCHUSTER
A VIACOM COMPANY

First published in Great Britain by Simon and Schuster, 1998
A Viacom Company

Simon and Schuster Limited
West Garden Place
Kendal Street
London W2 2AQ

Weight Watchers and *1,2,3 **Success Plus*** are Trademarks of Weight Watchers
International, Inc. and used under its control by Weight Watchers (U.K.) Ltd.

Design: Moore Lowenhoff
Cover design: Design in Mind
Typesetting: Stylize
Photography: Steve Lee
Styling: Marian Price
Food preparation: Wendy Lee

Weight Watchers Publications Manager: Juliet Hudson
Weight Watchers Publications Assistant: Celia Whiston

A CIP catalogue record is available from the British Library

ISBN 0 68481 978 3

Printed in Hong Kong

Pictured on the front cover: *Lamb Kebabs with Mint, Lime and Yogurt Marinade*
(page 26)

Pictured on the back cover: *Fruit and Rice Brûlée (page 46)*

Recipe notes:
Egg size is medium, unless otherwise stated.
Vegetables are medium-sized, unless otherwise stated.
It is important to use proper measuring spoons, not cutlery, for spoon measures.
1 tablespoon = 15 ml; 1 teaspoon = 5 ml
Dried herbs can be substituted for fresh ones, but the flavour may not always
be as good. Halve the fresh herb quantity stated in the recipe.

V shows the recipe is suitable for vegetarians

Contents

Introduction

I f you love food full of punchy flavours then grilling is definitely for you. It can make something really delicious out of a quite ordinary ingredient; compare the sweet, succulent taste of grilled peppers to raw peppers or peppers cooked by any other method. Grilling has the added advantage of being really quick and easy – ideal for after-work cooking.

Grilling is good for you!

It's a perfect cooking method for anybody on a diet. It doesn't require any extra fat and in some cases it can actually reduce the amount of fat in your food! When you grill sausages and bacon, for example, some of the fat runs out into the grill-pan.

It's such a quick method of cooking that your food loses very little in the way of vitamins.

Good Grilling

Many of us have experience of a barbecue where the food was charred on the outside and cold and raw on the inside. Most of us know how our grill behaves at different settings so we can avoid disasters like that, but to help you judge more accurately, guidelines and timings for grilling meat and fish are given on page 20.

The danger with grilling is that often your ingredients may dry out as they cook, so they need protection of some sort. Many recipes suggest brushing with oil or butter – not always practical if you are on a diet! Fortunately there are plenty of other solutions. You can keep fish, meat and poultry tender and juicy by starting them off under a hot grill to seal the outside and then reduce the heat (or move the food further away) to cook right the way through.

Low-fat oil sprays can also keep foods moist during grilling. These are widely available and if you just spray your food once or twice you won't use any Points. You can even make your own low-fat oil spray with a clean spray bottle and your favourite oil.

If you've marinated your ingredients then the marinade will help protect them from the heat of the grill. You can brush on any remaining marinade as a baste while the food cooks. Lemon and lime juice, and low-fat plain yogurt make excellent bases for marinades and have the added bonus that they will help to make meat more tender.

What to use

Generally speaking the recipes in this book assume you will be using the grill on your cooker, but many dishes are equally delicious cooked on the barbecue.

Some recipes are ideally suited to a ridged grill-pan, griddle or girdle. Traditionally griddles or girdles were used for baking Scotch pancakes, crumpets and Welsh cakes, but now ridged cast-iron or aluminium griddles can be used for all types of food and have the added bonus of giving an attractive striped appearance making it seem as if the food has been barbecued. Electric contact grills work on a similar principle to griddles and girdles – the food is in direct contact with the hotplate.

I have indicated in the recipes which cooking methods are suitable.

Barbecuing

Barbecues are great fun for the family and a wonderful way to entertain (providing the weather keeps fine). There are many types of barbecue on the market from simple small Japanese 'hibachi' types to sophisticated gas kettle barbecues. Do bear in mind basic safety rules.

What to serve with grills

Fresh vegetable sauces and fresh fruit and vegetable salsas are excellent low-Point accompaniments. You'll find recipes for these throughout the book. A small grill (meat or vegetables), served with a salad, is ideal for a quick snack and can be easily transformed into a more substantial meal by adding potatoes, bread, pasta or rice and hot vegetables.

Grilled Vegetables

Mediterranean countries have had an enormous influence on grilled vegetarian food and Mediterranean vegetables are ones which grill to great advantage. Peppers, aubergines, courgettes and tomatoes take on a wonderful smoky flavour after the skins have been charred under a medium grill. When the skin is removed, the resulting cooked vegetables have an intensity of flavour which bears little resemblance to that of the same vegetable in their raw state. Grilled pepper strips (page 12) and grilled mixed vegetables (page 8) can be eaten hot or cold and benefit from being tossed in a delicately flavoured salad dressing. And best of all, not only will your grilled vegetables taste delicious, most will also have 0 Points.

The term, 'au gratin', means a crunchy topping that can be added to many dishes. My version is a mixture of equal parts of breadcrumbs (either wholemeal or white), and grated half-fat cheese. This is ideal for vegetarian dishes. In fact cheese toppings are always good for grilling as they give a lovely golden-brown finish to the dish.

If you are cooking a barbecue for both vegetarians and meat eaters, make sure that the vegetarian food is kept right away from the meat, preferably on a different grill. Alternatively you could wrap either the meat or the vegetarian food in foil while it is cooking.

Mexican Rabbit

This is a Welsh rabbit with a Mexican flavour. Make it as hot as you like by adding more Tabasco or chilli sauce. A few lettuce leaves and a wedge of lime would be a cooling accompaniment.

Serves: 1
Preparation and cooking time: 15 minutes
Freezing: not recommended
Points per serving: 3¹/₂
Calories per serving: 200

1 medium slice of brown or white bread
40 g (1¹/₂ oz) half-fat Cheddar, grated
a few drops of Tabasco or chilli sauce
¹/₄ red pepper, de-seeded and chopped finely
a little skimmed milk

Ⓥ if using vegetarian Cheddar

❶ Preheat the grill.
❷ Toast the bread. Leave the grill on.
❸ Put the grated Cheddar in a basin and add the Tabasco or chilli sauce, red pepper and enough milk so that the mixture will spread easily.
❹ Spread the cheese mixture on the toast right to the edges.

❺ Toast under a hot grill until brown and bubbling.

Cook's note: a glass of chilled, spiced tomato juice would have a cooling effect as well.

Bruschetta with Grilled Vegetables

Bruschetta is the name given to toasted ciabatta, the popular Italian bread, but you can use other types of open-textured bread. Choose one or two of your favourite sorts of grilled vegetables for a delicious snack.

Serves: 2
Preparation time: 30 minutes salting + 10 minutes + 15 minutes cooking
Freezing: not recommended
Points per serving: 4^1/$_2$
Total Points per recipe: 9
Calories per serving: 280

Ⓥ

choose 2 or 3 from the following: aubergine, red pepper, yellow pepper, large courgette, fennel bulb, 4 shallots or 1 medium red onion
low-fat oil spray
2 tablespoons olive oil
juice of 1 lemon
1 garlic clove, sliced (optional)
2 thick slices of continental bread
salt and freshly ground black pepper

❶ Prepare the vegetables. For aubergines, slice them lengthways and sprinkle them with salt. Leave for 30 minutes. This will draw out excess water and give a better texture. Rinse thoroughly after salting and pat dry. Cut peppers and courgettes in half lengthways. For fennel, cut off the stalk ends, retaining the ferny leaves for a garnish. Slice lengthways so that sections are held together by the base of the stem. Peel and halve shallots. Peel and cut onion into eighths.

❷ Heat the grill to medium and spray vegetables with a little low-fat oil spray and season.
❸ Cook for 10–15 minutes, turning occasionally.
❹ Put on a warmed serving plate and sprinkle with oil and lemon juice and the sliced garlic clove (if using).
❺ Toast the bread on both sides and pile the vegetables on top.

Cook's note: a ridged grill/griddle gives an attractive finish to this dish.

Bean and Herb Cakes

There are so many fresh herbs available throughout the year now, that there is no excuse for bland food.
These cakes are delicious served with the Tomato and Chilli Sauce (page 41) or with the
Red Onion and Apple Marmalade (page 40).

Makes: 4 cakes
Preparation and cooking time: 25 minutes
Freezing: recommended
Points per cake: 2¹/₂
Total Points per recipe: 10
Calories per cake: 100

V if using a free-range egg

420 g can of cannellini beans, drained
1 onion, grated
2 garlic cloves, crushed
1 tablespoon chopped fresh mint (or dried mint)
1 tablespoon chopped fresh basil (or dried basil)
1 egg, beaten
3 tablespoons dried breadcrumbs
low-fat oil spray
salt and freshly ground black pepper

① Crush the beans with a potato masher.
② Add the onion, garlic, herbs, beaten egg, 1 tablespoon breadcrumbs and seasoning.
③ Leave to stand for 5 minutes.
④ Divide the mixture into four. Shape into 4 round cakes about 2.5 cm (1 inch) thick.
⑤ Coat the cakes with the remaining breadcrumbs.
⑥ Preheat the grill to medium.
⑦ Spray the cakes with oil and grill for 5 minutes on each side.

Cook's notes: a food processor makes quick work of these cakes. Whizz up the herbs first, then the onion and garlic and lastly the canned beans. Stir in the egg and 1 tablespoon breadcrumbs by hand.

Variations: try butter beans, borlotti beans or even chick-peas.

Use any of your favourite herbs. Chopped chives and/or parsley are good alternatives.

Grilled Pepper Strips with Italian Dressing

The skins of the peppers burn black when they are grilled, which adds a delicious smoky flavour to the dish.
You can use green peppers, but the sweeter red and yellow peppers are better.

Serves: 4 as a snack or 2 as a main meal
Preparation time: 10 minutes + 15 minutes cooking
Freezing: not recommended
Points per serving: 0
Total Points per recipe: 0
Calories per serving: as a snack 45, as a main
    meal 90

Ⓥ

4 peppers, red or yellow or a mixture of the two
For the dressing:
grated zest and juice of 1/2 lemon
150 ml (1/4 pint) tomato juice
2 garlic cloves, crushed
1 tablespoon wine vinegar or 1 teaspoon
    balsamic vinegar
6 basil leaves, shredded
salt and freshly ground black pepper
To garnish:
basil leaves
spring onions, sliced

❶ Preheat the grill to high.

❷ Cut the peppers in half lengthways.

❸ Grill, cut-side up, for 3 minutes, then turn and grill for 3 minutes more. Turn the grill down to medium and continue grilling for a further 10 minutes until the skin is black and blistered.

❹ Put the peppers in a polythene bag and seal. Leave for 15 minutes or so while making the dressing.

❺ In a basin add the lemon zest to the tomato juice. Strain in the lemon juice. Add the crushed garlic, vinegar and basil. Season to taste.

❻ Remove the peppers from the bag. Discard the stalks and seeds. The charred skins should come off easily leaving the smoky flesh.

❼ Cut the peppers into strips. Pour over the dressing and garnish with the basil leaves and spring onions.

Variation: use any flavoured tomato juice as a base for the dressing e.g. tomato juice with Worcestershire sauce.

Any fresh herbs can be used, but basil gives the most authentic Italian flavour.

Stuffed Curried Mushrooms

Stuffing mixes are a good store cupboard standby. Use them instead of fresh breadcrumbs and also for making an 'au gratin' topping for grilled foods. They come in a variety of flavours and are very low in fat. Serve the mushrooms with a crisp green salad and Fromage Frais and Watercress Sauce (page 41).

Serves: 4
Preparation time: 20 minutes + 20 minutes cooking
Freezing: recommended
Points per serving: 3
Total Points per recipe: 12
Calories per serving: 180

Ⓥ

1 packet of stuffing mix (about 125 g/4¹/₂ oz)
3 rounded teaspoons curry paste, mild or strong
1 tablespoon mango chutney
4 large flat mushrooms
4 teaspoons vegetable oil

❶ Make up the stuffing according to the packet instructions.
❷ Stir in the curry paste and the chutney.
❸ Wipe the mushrooms. Chop the stalks and add to the stuffing.
❹ Put a teaspoon of oil in each mushroom.
❺ When the stuffing has stood for the required time, fill each mushroom with a layer of stuffing about 2.5 cm (1 inch) thick. Any leftovers can be made into 'cakes' and grilled separately.
❻ Preheat the grill to medium. Place the mushrooms about 15 cm (6 inches) below the heat and grill for about 20 minutes.

Grilled Aubergine Dip

Grilling the aubergine adds a delicately smoked flavour to this dip. Serve with hot pitta or naan bread and raw vegetables. Multiply the mixture by two or three if you are making this for a party.

Serves: 2
Preparation time: 10 minutes + 20 minutes cooking
Freezing: not recommended
Points per serving: ¹/₂
Total Points per recipe: 1
Calories per serving: 55

Ⓥ

1 large aubergine
juice of 1 lemon
2 tablespoons low-fat plain yogurt
1 garlic clove, crushed
1 tablespoon chopped mint
salt and freshly ground black pepper

❶ Preheat the grill to high. Grill the whole aubergine, turning occasionally until the skin is blistered and black, and the flesh is soft.
❷ When cool enough to handle, peel off the skin.
❸ Put the flesh in a basin and drain off any excess liquid.
❹ Mash with a fork and add the lemon juice, yogurt, garlic, mint and seasoning to taste.

Cook's notes: you can use a food processor or blender to purée the aubergine and other ingredients.

Variations: add some chopped, skinned and de-seeded tomatoes to the mixture. (To skin tomatoes pour boiling water over them, leave for 1 minute, then refresh under cold water. The skins will slip off easily.) Chopped onions can also be used.

Marinated Tofu and Vegetable Kebabs

Tofu is quite bland if eaten on its own, but readily absorbs other flavours, so be bold with your marinades. During cooking tofu firms up even more and takes on a meaty texture. Serve with steamed rice, a green leafy salad and Fromage Frais and Watercress Sauce (page 41) adding the extra Points.

Serves: 4

Preparation time: 10 minutes + 24 hours
    marinating + 10 minutes cooking

Freezing: not recommended

Points per serving: 1

Total Points per recipe: 4

Calories per serving: 80

Ⓥ

280 g (10 oz) firm tofu
8 brown mushrooms
8 cherry tomatoes
16 fresh bay leaves
For the marinade:
1 garlic clove, crushed
1 tablespoon chopped coriander
2.5 cm (1 inch) root ginger, peeled and grated
1 tablespoon dark soy sauce
1 tablespoon dry sherry or 1 tablespoon lemon or
    lime juice
1 tablespoon tomato purée
salt and freshly ground black pepper

❶ Drain the tofu and cut into 16 cubes. Leave to drain again.

❷ In a basin mix together the marinade ingredients.

❸ Add the tofu, cover and marinate for 24 hours or more in the fridge, turning occasionally.

❹ Remove the tofu, reserving any remaining marinade. Thread the cubes, mushrooms, tomatoes and bay leaves on to 4 skewers, starting and finishing each skewer with a mushroom.

❺ Brush the finished kebabs with marinade.

❻ Preheat the grill to medium and grill for 10 minutes.

Variations: peppers, baby sweetcorn, patty pan squashes and baby new potatoes can be used. All need some pre-cooking before threading on to the skewers or they will not cook in time.

Quorn™ and Pasta au Gratin

Quorn™ is ideal for dieters because it is so low in fat. The au gratin topping adds a crunchy texture.
Serve with a green vegetable or salad.

Serves: 4

Preparation time: 5 minutes + 20 minutes cooking

Freezing: recommended

Points per serving: 5¹/₂

Total Points per recipe: 22

Calories per serving: 275

115 g (4 oz) pasta shapes or macaroni
235 g packet of Quorn™ chunks
1 tablespoon vegetable oil
1 onion, chopped
200 g (7 oz) can of chopped tomatoes
1 tablespoon tomato purée
1 tablespoon chopped parsley
50 g (1³/₄ oz) flavoured coating breadcrumbs
50 g (1³/₄ oz) half-fat cheese, grated
salt and freshly ground black pepper

❶ Cook pasta according to the packet instructions. Drain and mix with the Quorn chunks in a basin.

❷ Heat the oil and gently fry the onion until cooked but not browned.

❸ Add the onion to the pasta and Quorn. Mix in the tomatoes and tomato purée.

❹ Stir in the parsley, season well, and transfer to an ovenproof dish.

❺ Mix the breadcrumbs and cheese together and sprinkle evenly over the dish.

❻ Preheat the grill to medium. Place the dish about 20 cm (8 inches) away from the heat. Grill until golden brown.

Variation: Use a small can of Weight Watchers from Heinz soup instead of the tomatoes and the tomato purée.

Onion Flatbreads

There is something satisfying about making bread. These flatbreads are the simplest breads to make.
No raising agent is used and there is no long rising or proving time. I have made the breads using both a griddle
and an ordinary grill and the results on the griddle are much better.
A heavy frying-pan could be used instead of a griddle.

Makes: 8 flatbreads
Preparation time: 15 minutes + 10 minutes cooking
Freezing: recommended
Points per flatbread: 2
Total Points per recipe: 16
Calories per flatbread: 150 each

Ⓥ

175 g (6 oz) wholemeal flour
175 g (6 oz) plain flour + extra for rolling out
1 teaspoon salt
2 teaspoons cumin powder or cumin seeds
1 large onion, grated or chopped very finely
about 250 ml (9 fl oz) water
low-fat oil spray
salt and freshly ground black pepper

❶ Put the flours, salt, cumin, onion, and seasoning in a mixing bowl and stir well.

❷ Add the water gradually until a soft, but not sticky dough is formed.

❸ Knead for about 10 minutes (or use the dough hook of an electric mixer).

❹ Cut into 8 pieces and roll each into a ball.

❺ Roll out to a thin circle about 15 cm (6 inches) in diameter. Spray one side with oil.

❻ Heat a griddle, heavy frying-pan or grill to medium heat.

❼ If using a griddle or frying-pan, place the flatbread oiled side down on the griddle or pan and cook for 4–5 minutes on each side, spraying the other side when you turn it. If using the grill, cook the flatbreads in a grill pan, without the wire tray with the oiled side facing up. After 4–5 minutes, turn and spray the other side. Grill for a further 4–5 minutes.

Cook's notes: the flatbreads are best eaten immediately. If they are going to be frozen, cool first under a damp teatowel. Grilling will give a slightly spotty appearance whereas griddling gives a more even colour.

Weight Watchers notes: flatbreads make an excellent base for a snack. Top with Grilled Pepper Strips (page 12), Chargrilled Prawns (page 36) or a yogurt and cucumber dip.

Meat, Poultry and Fish

Grilling is a fast and fierce method of cooking and usually only the best cuts of meat are suitable if the finished results are to be moist and tender. Some pre-cooking may be necessary for cheaper cuts. Marinating in a meat-tenderising medium, such as yogurt, also helps.

Fish, on the other hand, always gives tender results; the danger here is overcooking, which will dry the fish out.

The tables below give approximate timings for grilling different cuts of meat and various fish according to how you like them cooked. As good quality meat is relatively expensive, it is best to check on timings before preparing a meal.

Fish

Fish	Prep	Heat of grill	Timings
Cod steak or fillet	spray with oil	medium	5–6 minutes each side
Herring		high	3 minutes each side
Mackerel	slash skin	medium	6 minutes each side
Trout	spray with oil	high	3 minutes each side
Salmon steak or fillet		medium	4 minutes each side
Plaice or sole fillets	spray with oil	medium	2–3 minutes each side
Shell-on raw prawns		high	2 minutes each side
Monkfish tails	spray with oil	medium	5 minutes each side

Meat and Poultry

Cut of meat	Doneness	Heat of grill	Timings
Lamb cutlets	medium	high	3 minutes each side
Lamb chops	medium	high	4–5 minutes each side
Pork or veal chops	well done	high	5 minutes each side
Pork steaks	well done	high	4–5 minutes each side
Kidneys, halved	medium	high	3 minutes each side
Liver, 1 cm ($1/2$ inch) thick	medium	high	3 minutes each side
Beef steaks, 1 cm ($1/2$ inch) thick	rare	high	2 minutes each side
Beef steaks, " " "	medium	high	3 minutes each side
Beef steaks, " " "	well done	high	4 minutes each side
Beef steaks, 2.5 cm (1 inch) thick	rare	high	$2^1/2$–3 minutes each side
Beef steaks, " " "	medium	high	4 minutes each side
Beef steaks, " " "	well done	high	5–$5^1/2$ minutes each side
Boneless chicken breast	well done	medium	7 minutes each side
Chicken quarters	well done	medium	10 minutes each side
Sausages	well done	medium	5–7 minutes each side
Chipolatas	well done	medium	4–6 minutes each side

Pitta Sandwich with Grilled Chicken Strips

Serves: 2

Preparation and cooking time: 20 minutes + marinating

Freezing: recommended for cooked chicken strips

Points per serving: 6

Total Points per recipe: 12

Calories per serving: 290

2 medium boneless, skinless chicken breasts
2 rounded teaspoons tikka spice mix

juice of 1 lemon
1 tablespoon tomato purée
1 tablespoon low-fat plain yogurt
$^1/_2$ teaspoon salt
low-fat oil spray
2 medium pitta breads
2 tablespoons shredded lettuce
2 tablespoons chopped coriander leaves
salt and freshly ground black pepper

❶ Cut the chicken into strips about 1 cm ($^1/_2$ inch) thick and put in a shallow ovenproof dish.

❷ Add the tikka spice mix, lemon juice, tomato purée, yogurt and salt and stir well. Cover and leave to marinate for at least an hour.

❸ Pre-heat the grill to hot. Spray the dish with oil.

❹ Grill for 10 minutes, turning occasionally. It doesn't matter if the strips start to char on the outside – this adds to the flavour.

❺ Towards the end of the cooking time, toast the pitta on both sides.

❻ Cut the pitta in half and open up the pockets.

❼ Fill with chicken, lettuce and coriander leaves. Season to taste.

Weight Watchers note: serve the chicken with a salad or some spinach.

Tandoori Chicken on Pappads

Serves: 4

Preparation time: 5 minutes + marinating + 15 minutes cooking

Freezing: recommended for cooked chicken

Points per serving: 4$^1/_2$

Total Points per recipe: 18

Calories per serving: 225

2 tablespoons ready-made tandoori paste or spice mix
150 ml ($^1/_4$ pint) low-fat plain yogurt
1 teaspoon tomato purée
4 medium boneless, skinless chicken thighs, cut into bite-size pieces
low-fat oil spray
4 pappads

❶ Make up the tandoori marinade according to the packet instructions – usually with yogurt and tomato purée. In a shallow ovenproof dish, add the marinade to the chicken. Leave to marinate for at least an hour or overnight if possible.

❷ Preheat the grill to high. Spray the chicken with oil and grill for 10 minutes. Turn the pieces occasionally – they should have a charred appearance.

❸ Grill the pappads, according to the packet instructions.

❹ Top each pappad with chicken and serve.

Cook's note: pappads are Indian unleavened breads, rather like poppadoms, but they only require grilling for a minute or less on each side.

Variation: use mini pitta bread to make a tandoori chicken sandwich. Add 40 Calories per serving. The Points will remain the same.

Chicken Satay Skewers with Bean Dip

Satay is an Indonesian dish and can be made with any lean meat – chicken, beef, pork or lamb. The traditional accompaniment is a high-fat peanut sauce. This bean dip is full of Indonesian flavours without any extra oil or fat.

Makes: 16 skewers

Preparation and cooking time: 20 minutes +
   30 minutes marinating

Freezing: not recommended

Points per 4 skewer serving: 4

Total Points per recipe: 16

Calories per 4 skewers: 125

2 medium skinless, boneless chicken breasts
1 tablespoon dark soy sauce
1 garlic clove, crushed
1 tablespoon dry sherry

2.5 cm (1 inch) root ginger, grated
1 teaspoon sugar
For the dip:
2 garlic cloves
1 small onion
2.5 cm (1 inch) root ginger
2 tablespoons coriander leaves
400 g (14 oz) can of butter, flageolet, white haricot
   or cannellini beans, rinsed and drained
juice of 1 lemon
2 teaspoons dark soy sauce

① Cut each chicken breast lengthways into 8 strips and put in a shallow dish.

② Add the soy sauce, garlic, sherry, ginger and sugar and stir.

③ In a food processor or blender blend the garlic, onion and ginger. Add the coriander and process a moment longer. Add the beans, lemon juice and soy sauce and process. If you don't have a blender or food processor you can chop the garlic, onion, ginger and coriander finely by hand. Mash the beans with the lemon juice and soy sauce, and then stir in the remaining ingredients.

④ Thread the chicken onto thin wooden skewers.

⑤ Preheat the grill and grill the skewers for 3 minutes on each side. Serve with the dip.

Cook's notes: thin wooden skewers are found in the barbecue section of supermarkets. Soak in water for 5 minutes before using to prevent them burning. Satay can also be cooked on a barbecue or griddle.

Weight Watchers note: for a quick snack, serve the dip as a spread on toast or with a selection of fresh vegetable strips.

Grilled Chicken Breast with Crunchy Topping

Soy sauce and sesame seeds give this chicken a delicious oriental flavour.

Serves: 1
Preparation time: 10 minutes + 15 minutes cooking
Freezing: recommended
Points per serving: 5
Calories per serving: 230

1 tablespoon sesame seeds
1 teaspoon dark soy sauce
1 teaspoon sesame oil or vegetable oil
1 medium skinless, boneless chicken breast
1 small carrot, grated
1/2 green pepper, cut into thin strips
2 teaspoons lemon juice

1 Mix together the sesame seeds, soy sauce and oil.
2 Spread on both sides of the chicken breast.
3 Preheat the grill to medium. Grill for about 15 minutes, turning occasionally.
4 Mix the carrot and pepper and toss with the lemon juice.
5 Serve the chicken with the salad.

Variations: leave the chicken to cool and then slice thinly into a salad of young spinach leaves or rocket.

The cold chicken, grated carrot and pepper also make a delicious sandwich filling.

Liver, Kidney and Mushroom Kebabs

Liver and kidneys are ideal for Weight Watchers as they contain little or no fat. This is good with steamed rice, courgettes and carrots.

Serves: 1
Preparation and cooking time: 20 minutes
Freezing: recommended
Points per serving: 5
Calories per serving: 260

1 lamb's kidney, halved and cored
125 g (4 1/2 oz) lamb's liver, cut into bite-size pieces
4 medium mushrooms
2 tablespoons low-fat plain yogurt
1 teaspoon grainy or Dijon mustard

1 Thread the kidney, liver and mushrooms on to a skewer.
2 Mix the yogurt and mustard together and brush over the skewer.
3 Preheat the grill to medium. Cook for 10 minutes, turning frequently, brushing more yogurt mixture over the skewer as necessary.

Variation: chicken livers can be used instead of lamb's liver. This will make the Calories per serving 205. The Points will be the same.

Grilled Chicken Breast with Crunchy Topping

Mini Mustard Beefburgers with Grilled Courgettes

Home-made burgers are so much more delicious than ready-made ones. They are quick to prepare and you can add the flavours you like best.

Makes: 4 burgers
Preparation time: 10 minutes + 15 minutes cooking
Freezing: recommended (see note)
Points per serving: 2½
Total Points per recipe: 10
Calories per serving: 185; with bun, 305

250 g (9 oz) extra-lean minced beef
50 g (1¾ oz) wholemeal flour
3 teaspoons grainy or French mustard
1 egg, beaten
2 courgettes
salt and freshly ground black pepper

❶ Put the meat, flour, 2 teaspoons mustard, egg and seasoning in a basin and mix together well.

❷ Divide the mixture into four and pat into burger shapes.

❸ Cut the courgettes in half lengthways and spread the cut side with the remaining mustard.

❹ Preheat the grill to medium. Grill the burgers and courgettes together for 15 minutes. Turn frequently. The burgers should be well cooked. Press them with the flat of a knife – no pink juices should come out.

Cook's notes: these are ideal for barbecues but keep them away from really fierce heat.

Weight Watchers note: choose extra-lean minced beef which has less than 10% fat (look at the nutritional information) or mince some lean stewing beef.

Variations: try serving the burgers in wholemeal buns.

You can substitute minced lamb for the beef; flavour with mint sauce rather than mustard. The Points will be 4½ per burger. The Calories will be 200 per serving.

Breadcrumbs, ground rice or semolina can all be used instead of flour; Points will remain the same.

Freezing note: you can freeze the uncooked burgers as long as the meat is fresh and not frozen.

Mini Mustard Beefburger with Grilled Courgettes

Sausage Patties with Leek and Orange Salsa

This is a versatile recipe. Different herbs can be used. And, instead of dividing the mixture into patties you could make a meatloaf; use a lightly oiled and crumbed 450 g (1 lb) loaf tin, sprinkle the top with more crumbs and bake it at Gas Mark 6/200°C/400°F for about 30 minutes. Drain away any fat and serve hot or cold, and cut into slices. Alternatively you could use the mixture as a stuffing for turkey or chicken. Serve with a green vegetable or salad.

Serves: 4
Preparation time: 10 minutes + 15 minutes cooking
Freezing: recommended for patties only
Points per 2 patty serving: 5
Total Points per recipe: 20
Calories per 2 patty serving: 225

8 low-fat sausages or 450 g (1 lb) low-fat sausage meat
1 small onion, grated
1 small eating apple, peeled and grated
1 tablespoon chopped fresh sage or 1 teaspoon dried sage
50 g (1³/₄ oz) fresh breadcrumbs
salt and freshly ground black pepper
For the salsa:
segments of 1 orange, pith and skin removed
1 small leek, sliced thinly

1 If you are using sausages then first skin them – straight from the fridge is best – and put the sausage meat in a mixing bowl.

2 Add the onion, apple and sage.

3 Add half the breadcrumbs and seasoning.

4 Mix together until smooth and divide into 8 equal pieces.

5 Roll each piece into a ball with wetted hands and flatten slightly.

6 Coat with the remaining breadcrumbs.

7 Cook under a medium grill for about 7 minutes on each side, turning occasionally.

8 Chop the orange segments roughly and put in a serving bowl with the juices. Add the leek and season.

Weight Watchers note: try serving the patties in a bun, hamburger-style, with the salsa on top. Remember to add the extra Points.

Salmon Steaks with Basil and Chunky Onion and Tomato Sauce

A lovely summer recipe to make when the tomatoes are ripe – ideal for cooking on the barbecue too.

Serves: 4

Preparation time: 15 minutes + 20 minutes cooking

Freezing: recommended (see note)

Points per serving: 3^1/$_2$

Total Points per recipe: 14

Calories per serving: 295

For the sauce:

250 g (9 oz) ripe tomatoes

1 large onion

1 tablespoon olive oil

1 garlic clove, crushed

salt and freshly ground black pepper

For the salmon:

low-fat oil spray

4 medium salmon steaks

grated zest and juice of 1 lemon

1 bunch of basil leaves, shredded

salt and freshly ground black pepper

❶ Pour boiling water over the tomatoes. Leave for 2 minutes and then drain and peel off the skins.

❷ Slice the onion thickly and cut the slices in half.

❸ Heat the oil in a small pan and add the onion and garlic. Cook slowly until softened but not browned (about 15 minutes).

❹ Cut the tomatoes in half and discard the pips. Chop the flesh roughly.

❺ Add the tomatoes to the pan and cook for a further 5 minutes. Season to taste.

❻ Spray four squares of foil with oil and place a salmon steak on each.

❼ Season well and sprinkle with the lemon zest, juice and basil. Close up the salmon parcels.

❽ Preheat the grill to high. Cook the salmon for 6 minutes. Open up the parcels and grill for 2 minutes more to brown the surface. There is no need to turn.

❾ Serve the steaks with the sauce in a separate jug.

Cook's notes: the onion and garlic can be softened in a microwave – 4 minutes on high. The timings in the recipe will produce fish that is lightly cooked and moist. If you prefer your fish well done, cook for 2 minutes more before opening up the parcels.

Variations: most fish can be grilled in this way as the foil protects the delicate flesh. Try mackerel, herring and salmon fillets, and whole red mullet.

Freezing note: freeze salmon and sauce separately.

Pork Steaks with Teriyaki Sauce

This Japanese-style marinade and sauce is a delicious way to prepare pork. Pork steaks can be trimmed so that they have very little fat. If you are cooking for more than one person, simply multiply the ingredients.

Serves: 1
Preparation time: 10 minutes + 1 hour marinating
   + 15 minutes cooking
Freezing: recommended
Points per serving: 5
Calories per serving: 150

1 medium pork steak, trimmed of fat
For the teriyaki marinade:
1 tablespoon dark soy sauce
1 garlic clove, crushed
1 cm (1/2 inch) root ginger, grated or chopped finely
1 tablespoon sherry, or mirin sauce
1 tablespoon apple or lemon juice

❶ Put the steak in a shallow ovenproof dish. Mix together the marinade ingredients. Add to the steak and leave to marinate for at least an hour.
❷ Preheat the grill to medium. Grill for about 15 minutes, turning frequently.
❸ Serve with the sauce, which will have thickened during cooking.

Cook's notes: this is an ideal recipe for barbecues – you may want to make extra sauce to accompany the barbecued steaks.

   Root ginger can be stored in the freezer. Grate the frozen ginger when you need it and return the rest to the fridge.

   You can also buy teriyaki sauce in the supermarket. It is found near the soya sauce.

Variations: try skinless chicken breasts instead of pork steaks. The Calories per serving will be 135 and the Points per serving will be 2$1/2$.

   Leave the cooked pork to cool, then cut into slices and add to a salad or use as a sandwich filling, along with some salad.

Pork Steak with Teriyaki Sauce

Salade Niçoise with Fresh Grilled Tuna

This traditional salad from Nice can also be made with canned tuna. But try to take advantage of the delicious fresh tuna which is widely available from most fishmongers and supermarkets.

Serves: 4
Preparation and cooking time: 20 minutes
Freezing: not recommended
Points per serving: 2¹/₂
Total Points per recipe: 10
Calories per serving: 160

2 Little Gem lettuces
4 tomatoes, sliced
115 g (4 oz) french beans
50 g (1³/₄ oz) black olives
2 hard-boiled eggs, sliced
50 g (1³/₄ oz) can of anchovies
175 g (6 oz) fresh tuna steak
the juice of 1 lemon
salt and freshly ground black pepper

❶ Put the lettuce leaves and tomatoes in a serving bowl.

❷ Pour boiling water over the french beans. Leave for 2 minutes and drain. Add to the bowl. Add the olives and eggs.

❸ Drain the oil from the anchovies and reserve 1 tablespoon. Snip the anchovies into 1 cm (¹/₂ inch) lengths and add to the salad.

❹ Preheat the grill to its highest setting. Season the tuna and grill for 2–3 minutes on each side (cook it longer if you prefer the fish well cooked).

❺ Cut the fish into strips and add to the salad.

❻ Make a dressing with the anchovy oil and the lemon juice. Season and pour the dressing over the salad.

Cook's notes: a cast-iron griddle is the ideal way to cook tuna; it sears the outside but leaves the centre still a little pink.

Variations: you can use any combination of raw vegetables for this salad. I have sometimes used samphire. This crunchy plant, which grows on the Norfolk coast, goes well with tuna – you can find it in fishmongers in the summer.

If you prefer, leave out the anchovies and make the dressing with a tablespoon of olive oil instead. The Calories will remain the same and the Points per serving will be 2.

Grilled Herring with Herb Stuffing

Parsley, coriander, dill or tarragon are particularly good in this recipe but you can use any type of herb.

Serves: 1
Preparation and cooking time: 20 minutes
Freezing: recommended before cooking
Points per serving: 6
Calories per serving: 200

3 tablespoons chopped fresh herbs + extra
    sprigs to garnish
1 small onion, chopped finely
1 lemon
1 medium herring, filleted (see Cook's notes)
salt and freshly ground black pepper

1 Mix together the herbs, onion and the juice of ½ lemon. Season well.

2 Spread the stuffing on one half of the herring and fold the other half over. Fasten with wooden cocktail sticks. Slash the skin on each side three times to prevent bursting.

3 Preheat the grill to medium. Cook for 5 minutes on each side.

4 Serve with the other half of the lemon and garnish with fresh sprigs of herbs.

Cook's notes: ask the fishmonger to fillet the herring and remove the head. Before you cook it, rinse it in cold water and pat dry.

    The fish can be wrapped in double foil and cooked on a barbecue for about 10 minutes.

Variations: small mackerel or trout are also excellent cooked like this. The Calories per serving for a small mackerel in this recipe will be 230 and the Points per serving will be 10; for trout the Calories per serving will be 200 and the Points per serving will be 3.

Chargrilled Prawns on Aubergine Slices

Serves: 2 as a main course or 4 as a starter or snack
Preparation and cooking time: 15 minutes + 30 minutes standing
Freezing: recommended for cooked aubergine slices
Points per serving: as a main course 1; as a starter or snack ½
Total Points per recipe: 2
Calories per serving: as a main course 45; as a starter 25

1 aubergine
2 tablespoons salt
1 teaspoon garam masala (optional)
low-fat oil spray
115 g (4 oz) raw prawns in their shells, defrosted if frozen
1 lemon, cut into wedges

1 Cut the aubergine lengthways into 5 mm (¼-inch) slices. Salt each slice and leave in a colander or sieve for 30 minutes at least. Rinse thoroughly and pat dry. Sprinkle with garam masala.

2 Preheat the grill to hot.

3 Spray the aubergine with oil. Grill for 5 minutes on each side. At the same time, grill the prawns on both sides until the shells start to char.

4 Divide the prawns between the slices of aubergine and serve with a wedge of lemon.

Cook's notes: you could also use a cast-iron griddle or use your barbecue. Garam masala is an aromatic mixture of spices often used in curries and Indian cooking. You'll find it with all the usual dried spices in your local supermarket.

Toasted Sandwiches

Sandwiches are one of the most popular snack meals and toasted sandwiches are particularly tasty. If you have an electric toasted-sandwich maker you can use all sorts of fillings which will not ooze out as the edges are sealed but bear in mind that ingredients such as lettuce will not heat well.

Make up the sandwich and press down well. Spray with oil, if you wish. Preheat the grill to high. Toast on both sides until golden brown.

As well as wholemeal or white bread, try pitta breads – these toast really well. French bread is also good and can be used when it is past its peak of freshness. The popular Italian ciabatta in all its variations makes good sandwiches, especially for continental-style fillings.

Even low-fat spreads contain some fat so, if you can, try not to use any. If you are using sliced bread, spray with a little low-fat oil spray before grilling. However all these fillings should melt pleasingly as they grill and keep the bread nice and moist. The ideas here will be sufficient for one round of sandwiches i.e. 2 slices of bread. **The Points are for fillings only so be sure to include extra Points for the sort of bread you use.**

Meat fillings:

- 25 g (1 oz) lean shaved meat (beef or pork) + 1 sliced tomato + 1 teaspoon grainy mustard:
  1 Point per serving. The Calories per serving will be 60.
- 25 g (1 oz) low-fat pâté + 1 teaspoon mango chutney + 1 tablespoon low-fat plain yogurt + chopped mint or parsley: 1 Point per serving. The Calories per serving will be 70.
- 25 g (1 oz) grilled lean ham or steak + 2 thin slices of raw onion + antipasti peppers:
  1 Point per serving. The Calories per serving will be 60.

Fish fillings:

- 1 rollmop herring + 1/2 eating apple, chopped + 1 tablespoon low-fat plain yogurt + chopped dill or parsley: 3 1/2 Points per serving. The Calories per serving will be 180.
- 25 g (1 oz) smoked salmon or salmon trout + 2 slices of lemon + 1 tablespoon low-fat soft cheese:
  1/2 Point per serving. The Calories per serving will be 55.
- 25 g (1 oz) shelled prawns or shrimps + 1 tablespoon low-fat mayonnaise + 4 slices of cucumber:
  1 1/2 Points per serving. The Calories per serving will be 70.

Cheese fillings:

- 25 g (1 oz) half-fat grated Cheddar + 3 chopped dates + 1 tablespoon pickle: 4 Points per serving. The Calories per serving will be 130.
- 25 g (1 oz) low-fat soft cheese + 1 pineapple slice (fresh or canned) + 1 celery stalk, chopped:
  1 Point per serving. The Calories per serving will be 55.
- 1 low-fat cheese slice + 2 rashers of lean bacon, grilled + 1 tablespoon tomato chutney:
  7 Points per serving. The Calories per serving will be 155.

Vegetable fillings:

- 2 tablespoons chopped fresh spinach + 4 thinly sliced mushrooms + 2 teaspoons olive oil:
  2 Points per serving. The Calories per serving will be 105.
- 2 sliced tomatoes + 1 tablespoon chopped basil leaves + 2 teaspoons tapenade (olive paste):
  2 Points per serving. The Calories per serving will be 40.

Marinades and Sauces

There are three main reasons to use marinades: they keep foods juicy and succulent, they help to tenderise tougher foods and they add flavour.

Grilling is a dry method of cooking and so very often grilled foods benefit from being marinated before cooking. Any leftover marinade can be used as a baste during cooking and can be thickened afterwards to make a sauce.

Because grilling is a quick method of cooking, the most suitable ingredients are tender foods, such as fish or the more tender cuts of meat. However, tougher foods can be tenderised by marinating with acid ingredients such as yogurt, lemon juice or vinegar.

Sauces and marinades also add flavour. Mildly flavoured foods, such as Quorn™, tofu, and, to some extent, chicken can be enlivened by marinating with well-flavoured ingredients. Most cuisines have examples of this: in India the signature flavours are cumin, turmeric and coriander; in Thailand lemon grass, lime, ginger and coconut; in Italy tomatoes, basil and garlic; in Provence onions, herbs, tomatoes and olives and in Mexico chilli and tomato.

Ready-prepared sauces and marinades make life easier but you still need to allow time for the marinade to do its job – at least an hour and preferably overnight in a cool place.

As well as the recipes in this chapter, you'll find other sauce and marinade recipes in this book, so do experiment.

Yogurt Marinade

Because of its acidity and bland flavour, yogurt makes a good base for a tenderising marinade. It is particularly good with salmon, mackerel and herring. It's also delicious with lamb steaks or chops or on kebabs.

Serves: 4
Preparation time: 5 minutes
Freezing: not recommended
Points per serving: ¹/₂
Total Points per recipe: 2
Calories per serving: 25

ⓥ

125 ml (4 fl oz) tub of low-fat plain yogurt
1 garlic clove, crushed
1 tablespoon chopped coriander leaves
1 teaspoon cumin
grated zest and juice of 1 lemon or lime
salt and freshly ground black pepper

❶ Mix together the yogurt, garlic, coriander and cumin in a bowl. Stir in the grated zest and juice and season.

Cook's notes: you can add other flavourings to complement your main ingredient. After marinating, leave the coating of yogurt on the food as it gives a lovely spicy, crusty finish.

It is preferable to leave meat for at least 2 hours to marinate (and tenderise), preferably overnight. Fish only needs to be marinated for 1 hour.

Melon and Cucumber Salsa

A salsa is an uncooked chunky sauce made with fresh fruit and/or vegetables. It's a light, refreshing accompaniment to grilled meat or fish.

Serves: 4
Preparation time: 10 minutes
Freezing: not recommended
Points per serving: 1/2
Total Points per recipe: 2
Calories per serving: 40

V

1/4 **Galia melon or any green or yellow-fleshed melon, cut in small cubes**
1 **small onion, chopped finely**
1/2 **cucumber**
2 **tablespoons chopped mint**
1 **teaspoon vinegar or lemon juice**
salt

❶ Put the melon in a bowl. Add the onion.
❷ Peel the cucumber and cut in half lengthways. Scoop out the seeds and cut into cubes. Add to the melon.
❸ Add the mint, vinegar or lemon juice and salt to taste. Serve separately from the grilled food.

Variations: choose other herbs to complement your main ingredient. Parsley or dill would be ideal with fish; fresh coriander or tarragon would suit chicken.
Add a chopped, de-seeded beefsteak tomato to the basic mixture.

Red Onion and Apple Marmalade

Although it takes some time to cook this thick sauce, it freezes well and will keep in the fridge for about a week. It is versatile and adds lots of flavour to grilled foods.

Serves: 6
Preparation time: 10 minutes + 45 minutes cooking
Freezing: recommended
Points per serving: 1/2
Total Points per recipe: 3
Calories per serving: 40

450 g (1 lb) **red onions, cut into 1 cm (1/2 inch) slices**
2 **dessert apples, peeled and sliced**
3 **tablespoons chicken stock**
2 **tablespoons balsamic or wine vinegar**
2 **teaspoons brown sugar**

❶ Preheat the grill to low. Grill the onion slices for about 20 minutes, turning occasionally until softened and slightly charred at the edges.
❷ Chop coarsely and put in a pan with the remaining ingredients.
❸ Bring to the boil and simmer for 20 minutes or until the apples are soft. Serve hot or cold.

Cook's notes: instead of grilling the onions, you can cook them slowly in a covered pan with the stock for 20 minutes before adding the other ingredients.
Balsamic vinegar gives a richer flavour and colour than wine vinegar. Do use it if you can.

Variation: ordinary onions work fine for this recipe but the red ones do have a better flavour.

Fromage Frais and Watercress Sauce

This recipe couldn't be easier. It has a lovely fresh green appearance and it's versatile too. Serve with simply grilled meat, poultry or fish or use as a dressing for potato or pasta salad. A food processor makes fast work of chopping the watercress.

Serves: 4
Preparation time: 5 minutes
Freezing: not recommended
Points per serving: $^1/_2$
Total Points per recipe: 2
Calories per serving: 30

V if using vegetarian fromage frais

1 large bunch of watercress, chopped finely
200 g (7 oz) tub of very-low-fat plain fromage frais
salt and freshly ground black pepper

1 Stir together the watercress and fromage frais and season to taste.

Variation: use baby spinach leaves or rocket instead of the watercress.

Tomato and Chilli Sauce

This is a useful standby for all types of grilled meats and vegetables – it's particularly good with barbecues. Meats can also be casseroled in this sauce for a good winter warmer.

Serves: 6
Preparation time: 15 minutes + 20 minutes cooking
Freezing: recommended
Points per serving: $^1/_2$
Total Points per recipe: 3
Calories per serving: 55

V if using vegetarian Worcestershire sauce

1 tablespoon oil
1 onion, chopped finely
2 garlic cloves, crushed
$^1/_2$ teaspoon chilli powder
2 tablespoons wine vinegar
3 tablespoons Worcestershire sauce
2 tablespoons tomato purée
1 tablespoon honey
$^1/_2$ teaspoon mustard powder or 1 teaspoon ready-made mustard
200 g (7 oz) can of chopped tomatoes
salt

1 Heat the oil in a small saucepan and gently cook the onion, garlic and chilli powder for about 5 minutes until soft, but not browned.
2 Add all the other ingredients and bring to the boil. Simmer without a lid for 20 minutes. Serve immediately.

Weight Watchers notes: artificial sweetener can be used instead of the honey but add this just before serving. Do not heat the sauce again or the flavour will be bitter.

Desserts

t may come as a surprise but grilling is an ideal way to produce a whole range of exciting desserts.

Naturally sweet fruit, like pineapple, grill well and even canned fruit in natural juice gives a good result. When the fruit is grilled, the natural sugar contained in the fruit caramelises, giving a toffee-like colour and flavour. Bananas should be grilled whole in their skins. A cooked banana is deliciously creamy.

A brûlée finish is very luxurious and adds a lovely crunch to desserts. It is always exciting to tap the brittle toffee top and find out what surprises are underneath.

Grilled Bananas

Nothing could be simpler than this recipe. Bananas which are a little past their best are ideal to use. It's a great barbecue dish as well.

Serves: 1

Preparation and cooking time: 10 minutes

Freezing: not recommended

Points per serving: with low-fat plain yogurt 1¹/₂;
with very-low-fat plain fromage frais 1¹/₂;
with 1 scoop of low-fat ice cream 2¹/₂;
with low-calorie jam 2

Calories per serving: with low-fat plain yogurt 120;
with very-low-fat plain fromage frais 120;
with 1 scoop of low-fat ice cream 150;
with low-calorie jam 120

Ⓥ

1 medium banana, unpeeled

1 tablespoon low-fat plain yogurt or very-low-fat plain fromage frais or 1 scoop of low-fat ice cream or 1 tablespoon low-calorie jam

❶ Preheat the grill to medium and put the unpeeled banana on the grill pan.

❷ Cook, turning occasionally for about 10 minutes. (The skin will turn quite black.)

❸ Remove carefully to a plate and with a sharp knife, cut a slit down the length of the banana. Peel back the skin carefully.

❹ Using the banana skin as a container, mix the yogurt, fromage frais, ice cream or jam with the cooked banana.

Grilled Banana

Grilled Orchard Slices with Plum Sauce

In the autumn, when all these fruits are in season, this dish makes a change from the usual stewed fruit. Canned pears also grill well.

Serves: 4
Preparation and cooking time: 20 minutes
Freezing: not recommended
Points per serving: 1
Total Points per recipe: 4
Calories per serving: 60

2 medium apples
2 medium pears
juice of 1/2 lemon or 1 tablespoon orange juice
1 teaspoon mixed spice
250 g (9 oz) plums

Ⓥ

❶ Cut each apple across in 4 slices (do not remove the skin) and remove the core.
❷ Quarter the pears and remove the cores.
❸ Blend the juice and spice together and brush over the cut surfaces of the fruit.
❹ Put the plums and 2 tablespoons of water in a pan. Bring to the boil and simmer, covered, for 10 minutes or until the plums are soft.
❺ Preheat the grill to medium. Grill the fruit on foil for 10 minutes or until beginning to brown, turning occasionally.
❻ Rub the cooked plums through a sieve. Put a pool of sauce on each of four plates and arrange the apple and pear slices on top.

Cook's notes: do not be tempted to microwave whole plums. They will explode because of the stone inside. Halved and stoned plums can be microwaved.

Fresh Fruit Kebabs

Grilling intensifies the flavour of the fruit. This is a very easy dessert for a barbecue. Serve with Weight Watchers from Heinz ice cream or low-fat plain yogurt or fromage frais.

Serves: 4
Preparation and cooking time: 15 minutes
Freezing: not recommended
Points per serving: 1
Total Points per recipe: 4
Calories per serving: 45

1 small pineapple
100 g (3 1/2 oz) strawberries
100 g (3 1/2 oz) black grapes

Ⓥ

❶ Peel the pineapple and cut into wedges. Cut off the thick central core and cut the remaining flesh into bite-size pieces. Thread all the fruits on to 4 skewers.
❷ Preheat the grill to hot. Grill for 5 minutes, turning frequently.

Variations: try peach or nectarine slices, plum or apricot halves, apple or pear slices, orange or grapefruit segments.

Fresh Fruit Kebab

Fruit and Rice Brûlée

Brûlée means burnt. It refers to the topping which is a crisp layer of caramelised sugar.

Serves: 2
Preparation and cooking time: 10 minutes +
    2 hours chilling
Freezing: not recommended
Points per serving: 4
Total Points per recipe: 8
Calories per serving: 220

(v)

1/2 peach, sliced or 50 g (1³/₄ oz) berries
425 g (15 oz) can of Weight Watchers from Heinz
    rice pudding
2 tablespoons caster sugar

1 Divide the fruit between 2 ovenproof individual dishes.
2 Divide the rice pudding between the 2 dishes and refrigerate for at least 2 hours.
3 Preheat the grill to its highest setting.
4 Sprinkle the top of each dish with the sugar and stand the dishes on a baking sheet.
5 Grill until the sugar has melted and is golden brown. Allow to cool a little before eating.

Cook's notes: ramekins are ideal for this recipe, but if you don't have individual dishes, use any small ovenproof dish and make two portions in one dish.

Variations: you can also make brûlées with low-fat fromage frais or low-fat plain yogurt instead of rice pudding and any seasonal fruit can replace the peach or berries.

Grilled Pineapple with Cinnamon

This simple recipe is so versatile. It can be served hot or cold on its own or with Weight Watchers from Heinz ice cream, or with low-fat fromage frais or low-fat plain yogurt. It also makes a great accompaniment to grilled meats and is particularly good with gammon or pork.

Serves: 1
Preparation and cooking time: 15 minutes
Calories per serving: 30
Points per serving: 1
Freezing: not recommended

(v)

1 pineapple slice, about 1.5 cm (⁵/₈-inch) thick
1 tablespoon orange juice
1/2 teaspoon ground cinnamon

1 Put the pineapple in a small ovenproof dish or tin.
2 Blend the orange juice with the cinnamon and pour over the pineapple.
3 Preheat the grill to medium. Grill for about 4 minutes on each side, or until golden.

Cook's note: ready-prepared fresh pineapple rings make this dessert very quick and easy. Or you could use canned pineapple in natural juices.

Fruit and Rice Brûlée

Index